Sister Stanislaus Kennedy is an Irish Sister of Charity and the founder of Focus Ireland, the Inaugural Council of Young Social Innovation, Ireland, and the Sanctuary. She has been instrumental in developing and implementing social-service programmes that have benefited thousands of people in need throughout Ireland and Europe. For this work, she has received many awards, including Honorary Degrees of Law from Trinity College Dublin, the National University of Ireland and the Open University, as well as a presidential medal from New York University.

She has written four bestselling books, *Now is the Time*, *Gardening the Soul*, *Seasons of the Day* and *Stillness Through My Prayers*, and is currently working on her latest book.

D1248600

www.transworldireland.ie

www.**rbooks**.co.uk

Also by Sister Stan

SEASONS OF THE DAY
NOW IS THE TIME
GARDENING THE SOUL

and published by Transworld Ireland

Stillness

through my prayers

SISTER STAN

TRANSWORLD IRELAND

TRANSWORLD IRELAND
an imprint of The Random House Group Limited
20 Vauxhall Bridge Road, London SW1V 2SA
www.rbooks.co.uk

STILLNESS: THROUGH MY PRAYERS
A TRANSWORLD IRELAND BOOK: 9781848270619

First published in Great Britain and Ireland TownHouse, 2006
Transworld Ireland edition published 2009

Copyright © Sr Stanislaus Kennedy 2006

Addresses for Random House Group Ltd companies outside the UK
can be found at: www.randomhouse.co.uk
The Random House Group Ltd Reg. No. 954009

The Random House Group Limited supports The Forest Stewardship
Council (FSC), the leading international forest certification organisation.
All our titles that are printed on Greenpeace approved FSC certified
paper carry the FSC logo. Our paper procurement policy can be found at
www.rbooks.co.uk/environment

Text design by Sin É Design
Typeset in Adobe Garamond
Printed in the UK by CPI Bookmarque, Croydon, CR0 4TD

2 4 6 8 10 9 7 5 3 1

CONTENTS

beyond fear

Help me arise today like the morning sun, feeling safe, protected, watched over, cared for.

Help me arise today with courage to ascend beyond the fray, regardless of difficulties, threats assailing me, criticisms meeting me, knowing nothing can destroy the gift of who I am.

Help me make something of this day, before it is too late, before letting it go. Let me give myself to the joy of the day before leaving it.

To know the light we must know the dark.
To be full we must be empty.

Bring me comfort, bring me support, help me to feel safe, give me something to hold on to.

There is never a moment that isn't an opportunity to create something new.

There is never a moment when there isn't something to let go.

There is never a moment that isn't an opportunity to make space for the new by letting go of the old.

Grant me;
in time of fortitude, sturdiness;
in the face of loss, robustness;
in the face of difficulty, tenacity;
So that I can begin again in the face of adversity –
suffused with hope.

Help me believe that the pain of life, accepted
with courage, awakens love, stirs compassion,
melts my hardness, frees my creativity,
opens my mind.

Help me to listen to the quiet voice within, the unheard voices around me. There are voices speaking to me, teaching me, reminding me who it is I am, where it is I am going.

Help me to sift the viable from the moribund,
separate the gold from the dross, reflect on what
I need, what I can let go of before moving on.

When negativity is lurking, watching, waiting, it
is trying to take hold. Negativity faced,
acknowledged, confronted, named and claimed,
frees me to let it go.

Waiting in the darkness of blindness, helplessness and hopelessness calls forth faith and trust – a letting go, as I await God's coming.

Children delighting in bog, in swampy lands
where large water pools form.

Children in their wisdom teaching us to watch
and wait.

Nelson Mandela spent time – twenty-seven years
– locked up, waiting, imprisoned in darkness.
Waiting in darkness, he became light, shining for
his people, party, country, world.

Darkness faced alone – desolation, emptiness,
loneliness, confusion, fear.

Darkness accepted, faced with faith, hope, love –
new life born within us, bringing peace, courage,
vision.

In darkness, everything appears meaningless;
prayer valueless, God distant, people aloof, life
empty, inspiration absent.

Gazing on God in the sanctuary of my heart,
darkness invites me to know without
knowing anything.

It is in not knowing that I know.

My doubt – painful, embarrassing, confusing;
makes me feel failure, blocking my ability
to pray.

My Faith – struggling, striving, persisting; light in crisis, bringing me home to myself as I welcome the day.

Becoming myself, here, now, today. Growing, blossoming, blooming, blessing, radiating, peacefully, happily, joyfully, contentedly, satisfied with who I am.

Help me integrate the different facets of my life. Reduce the power of darkness over me, make the hostile hospitable, the strange familiar. Help me affirm life.

Boredom. Life force blocked, enthusiasm sapped, energy dissipated, feelings trapped, fears preventing me from experiencing joy.

By facing my fears, expressing my feelings, releasing my energy, feeling my enthusiasm, freeing my creativity, boredom dissipates and joy is recovered.

Suffering humanity. Alone. Not alone. Alone in
this suffering. Not alone in suffering.

Shadows follow me everywhere, every day.
Unrecognised, repressed, disowned, cast aside,
they frighten me.

Confronted, recognised, acknowledged, claimed
and named, they illuminate and guide me,
bringing comfort and peace.

Loneliness, a universal human condition.
With loneliness unacknowledged, I feel rejected,
denied, avoided. With loneliness faced, I feel
understood, accepted, at peace.

Living according to the expectations of others, we become a collection of masks, defined roles always looking for a challenge, a crisis to solve, someone to heal, something, anything to fill our inner emptiness.

Help me accept my emptiness, embrace my
aloneness. I grow and blossom, finding the person
I am called to be – my true self.

Help me to move beyond my fears, to move into
them, acknowledge, name, accept, confront,
discuss and talk them over until they dissipate,
disappear, lose their power over me.

By accepting myself and others, by allowing mine
and others' weaknesses transform me, I open to
the next moment with new awareness and a
new heart.

Creation reflected upon and prayed over leads to
gratitude as I discover a new power within me,
beyond me, present to me, nourishing me, serving
my every need, calling me to new depths
each day.

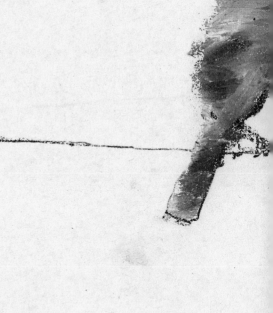

Negativity unacknowledged is draining, alluring, addictive, crippling, controlling.

Negativity faced, named, claimed brings awareness, peace, integrity, dignity, freedom, truth and happiness.

Living in the moment ensures I do not miss the
present or find it gone before I have
experienced it.

Lord, ensure I do not find the day has passed me
by before I have fully lived it. Help me greet the
night with gratitude. Help me welcome death
when its moment comes.

Fear acknowledged, accepted, honoured and
worked with is a way to my inner peace.

Help me to face the unseen with courage. Free me to look forward, believe in goodness, to meet and embrace each new day.

beyond fear

trust

Teach me to trust myself, to follow my deepest
desires, explore the recesses of my heart, as I strive
to become whole.

Faith is living with promise, with waiting, with darkness, with ambiguity, with uncertainty. Faith, a gentle strength without answers.

Believing goodness awaits us, we stop –
tasting its gift.

Believing life is flawed, we stop – feeling the fear.

Believing our soul is luminous, we stop –
discovering life's blessings.

Giving thanks, an outward trust. Teach me to become less concerned with what is missing and more focused on sharing what has been given to me this day.

Aspiring to good inspires others to goodness.

Aspiring to good, I pray now to reject
competitiveness, prejudice, judgement, hypocrisy,
cynicism, negativity, arrogance,
closed-mindedness, aggression.

Aspiring to good, I pray now to inspire others to
give, heal, forgive, with tenderness, openness,
affirmation, creativity, goodness.

In the evening, I lift my heart in gratitude for the gifts of the day and allow God's forgiveness flow through me into our world. Forgiveness in the evening brings peace at night.

I am called to see with eyes of faith, to leap in the
dark, to trust with the simplicity of a child and
surrender to God's protection.

My purpose this day is not seeking security and
certainty. It is discovering the very best that is
within me. Finding this, I find love, joy, freedom.

Opening to my inner self frees me to trust each new moment in time and calls me to attentive listening. Inviting me to hear that small voice deep inside, the voice of God.

Patient, waiting in silence, teaching me to believe
in myself, to hold nothing back, to accomplish
much and to transform problems into
possibilities.

Accepting myself with all my wounds and
forgiving myself and others, I become free,
empowered, without guile, without blame. God
give me the wisdom of maturity.

May I learn to accept and live with the polarities,
tensions, paradoxes, contradictions of our world.

May I learn to accept without understanding, find
unity in diversity, as I move through each day,
as I move through my life.

With gratitude and praise, I make peace with the
world, with everything in my life, not excusing or
ignoring but acknowledging everything as
part of me.

Facing the vulnerability of my humanness is the bedrock of truth.

Exposing the fragility of my humanness is the way of truth.

With reverence, I accept the mystery of truth.

trust

letting go

Sun sets, evening descends, light fades, day draws
to a close. I light a lamp and a new glow streams
across my day.

Hour of peace, silence falling on the world.

Setting aside the day, I enter into the serenity
of evening.

Resting in the peace of evening, conflicts and
contradictions are resolved by reflecting on the
fragility of my life, the changing face of the world.
I go forward in a spirit of quiet festivity, greeting
the silence of descending darkness.

Help me to learn to be present to the present, in
mindfulness, in recollection – the beginning of
serenity.

In the cool of the evening, I reflect on the gifts of the parting day.

In the quiet of night, teach me to listen to my
own silence, the unaccepted parts of myself, to the
silence around me, the silence of those in pain,
the silence of children, the silence of oppressed
people who dare not speak.

Sunrise never fails to surprise me. It flows through my senses, transforming me with lithesomeness, gracefulness, gratefulness.

God's miracles are everywhere.

The day is drawing to a close. It is time to offer what I have undone, done and left undone. It is time to let go, relinquish possession of the day. It is time to give back freely what I have been freely given.

letting go

Attentiveness takes on a new significance as it deepens my sense of wonder for everything.

Watching the last darkness of night sky dissipate.
Waiting as the sun filters through – another
miracle.

Giving myself over to sleep, acknowledging my
need for rest, is accepting my mortality.

In sleep, I believe that simply being is fruitful
in itself.

Twilight time; time between two worlds.
The frenzied world quietens, light recedes,
darkness deepens, the unhurried pace of the new
world takes over.

Dusk; indistinct, hazy and undefined. Our world
united in formlessness, the twilight of day, the
twilight of life.

Night, a time to forgive, radiate goodness, say good things, acknowledge the sacred, bless creation, call forth the best in all.

At night I come to know the mysteriousness of God. I come to know that God cannot be made in my image according to my way. I come to know that you, O God, are always shaping and creating me in your likeness.

Evening time brings me home to my true self.
It takes me beyond my ego, connecting me with
what lies beyond – a journey into the depth of my
inner being, a journey of soul and spirit.

As I name and claim my gifts, my blessings, I give
thanks for what is good in myself and in others,
and share with gladness the marvels of my day.
As I realise my potential, my gifts shine as
my blessings.

Draw me into the mystery of night as I gather together the day, offering it back to You in gratitude.

I recognise the universal rhythms of day and night, sunsets and moon rises, great movements of seas and stars, seasons and natural cycles.

I ponder in my heart creation's story, surrendering to the rhythms of day and night, month and year.

As shadows lengthen, time fades and day declines.
I stop, and looking back, I give thanks and
ask forgiveness.

I ask forgiveness; I give thanks.

stillness

July 2, 2009
1 Oledeler
Heneral Store
10:12 a.m.

As I put away the day, I prepare to rest, aware
there is a time for everything, a time to rest, as
surely as there is a time to work.

Surrendering to sleep, stepping out of the day
into night. Setting aside tasks not because they are
finished or accomplished, but because now it is
time to rest.

The silence of the night invites me to detach
myself from possession of the day. Entrusting it,
I entrust myself to the freedom of God.

As evening draws in and darkness falls, I am
reminded that life, work and creation will manage
without me until morning, and I let go of the day.

Night-time, reflecting on the day, being grateful,
forgiving, confronting fears with faith, looking
back, moving forward.

letting go

In darkness, light shines brightly. Knowing light,
I come to know darkness itself is light.

In the evening, I gather together my
contradictory, mixed-up day. Accepting it for what
it is, in all its imperfections, brings peace.

In the sacredness of the night, we move beyond what is visible, into the core of our being, where we realise we are known completely, loved unconditionally by our creator.

Now I give thanks and praise for what is given
and I remember what otherwise might go
unnoticed.

Gratitude in itself brings happiness. In time, we learn to give thanks for everything, loss and gain, conflict and peace, sorrow and joy, sickness and health. Gratitude always brings happiness.

Night, a time of surrendering, resting, waiting,
yielding to the transforming power of sleep.

Help me surrender to prayer, even when it seems empty of meaning, even when I have forgotten how to pray.

Draw me into the movement of night. As the sky changes and night falls, assist me to shift gear and to notice the greatness of God.

mystery

You, God of all the earth, God of Abraham and
Sarah, Isaac and Rebecca, Jacob and Rachel, are
beyond categories, beyond masculine and
feminine, are eternally unnamed. You are
eternal mystery.

When I think I have no time, that I am running
out of time, I imagine that time is out
of my control.

Time is eternal. We have all the time
we need, always.

God, seeking you with my mind, you slip my
grasp. Thinking I understand you, you change.
Believing I see you, you move ahead. Seeking you
in my heart, you reveal yourself to me, in truth.

God of my heart, create in me an awareness of the impermanence, transitoriness and limitations of the material world. Create in me an awareness of the permanence, endurance, timelessness of what is spiritual, what is eternal.

Creation; full of beauty, often hidden, abused,
tiny, fragile.

Creation; needing to be supported, protected,
acknowledged, appreciated, realised, loved
into being.

No one lives by chance. Everyone, everything has a purpose, a part to play, in the grand design that is creation.

This day offers me opportunities to accept,
discover, affirm, delight, in the uniqueness
that is me.

Help me on the journey of learning and discovering. Teach me not to fear uncertainty and vulnerability. Lead me to discover inner strength, peace, energy and joy.

Smell – a source of undiluted pleasure, joy unimagined, never merited, always available. The smell of freshly cut grass, ploughed fields, falling rain, morning dew, footed turf, mowed hay, salt water and of freshly baked bread. Pure gift, freely given to each of us, out of love.

Help me to discover and accept who I am and
what I am called to be. The purpose of this day is
to find the joy I was born to know, the person I
was born to be.

A day lived in unity with nature is a day lived as a circle, continuously flowing, in the eternal cycle of creation.

I give of my best when I am at my best. The more
life exhausts, drains, stresses, the less I give.
Unnatural rhythms overshadow me.

I offer my day to God.

Help me become less preoccupied with doing, more aware of being, less wrapped up in decisions, more in tune with my deep desires, less attentive to reason and logic, more attentive to my intuitions, less concerned with 'why', more open to discovering the mystery of life.

The more I bless, the more I am blessed.
Blessings never run out. They are drawn from a
bottomless source, replenished eternally.

Journeying towards the truth, living with questions, uncertainty, ambiguity. Secure in not knowing, never fully understanding, always seeking, never arriving. Answers becoming questions, questions answers.

Between dark and light.

Living now, not in the past, not in the brightness of light yet to come. Living here in this moment, experiencing contentment and peace.

The mystery of now.

Darkness is part of my journey into the gift of
life. In accepting darkness, may I perceive light,
learn to know beyond logic, beyond reason.

Wild flowers, caressing the earth with blessings.
Pulling them up, they grow again in unexpected
places; on pavements, rooftops, dying tree stumps.
They find a way through…

Trampling them underfoot, they find a way to
blossom and bless.

God of the clouds and sky, sun and moon, trees
and flowers, creatures of sky and sea, lakes and
rivers, mountains and hills, showers and rain, tears
and laughter, night and day, darkness and light,
breezes and wind, fire and water, air and earth.
Closer to us than we often imagine.

God, teach me what is sacred within my day as
I tread on holy ground.

God, always waiting to enlighten throughout the night. Jacob struggled with the angel of darkness. At dawn, the struggle finished and Jacob's angel blessed him with a disability. Entering into night, we too struggle with the angel of darkness, discovering our true selves at dawn. We are blessed to know that our weakness is our strength.

One journey, two paths:
the outer path – career, work, busyness;
the inner path – silence, stillness, hidden.
An integrated day – travelling both paths
at one time.

God beyond all my understanding. Bringing balance and harmony to the boundless resources, the powerful energies, the store of strength, the endless potential of my being – be my guide.

You invite me to journey into myself, into the
vast interior of my psyche, my soul, my heart. You
call me from safety, comfort, knowing, into the
unknown, into the dark, into You, into the sacred
space within.

Earth; strong, steady, serene, supportive.
Air; light and free, without form.
Fire; hot, bright, energetic.
Water; flowing, swerving.

Earth, air, fire and water; in me, around me, part
of me, protecting me, bringing me to a place
where I connect with myself, others and
the universe.

Miracle of humanity, remembering dust and earth. Breath of God, enfolding my nothingness, consecrating me, blessing me, reminding me that I am both human and divine.

At the core of our being, we are all one in the unity of creation. We are drawn together as we touch and are touched by each other. We are a centre of gravity in the heart of creation.

Help me on this journey towards wholeness –
never complete; uncovering, reclaiming,
gathering, integrating, discovering what is lost,
losing what is found. A journey of light
and darkness.

Journeying with awareness, with attention, with mindfulness. Each event is unique, each step the first step.

stillness

Accepting the mystery of our being. Not proving it, being it – I become the person I was meant to be, the self I was born to be.

My spiritual journey, the greatest human adventure – I am going beyond certainties, knowledge, understanding, doubts. I am always journeying towards an ever-unfolding truth.

truth

Sabbath, a space, a time, saying yes to the sacred.
Sabbath, a joy, a rest, never a burden,
never a chore.

truth

I count my blessings, recognising enough as enough, giving thanks for everything.

The way of truth tests my heart, examines my motivation, challenges my commitment, brings loving perseverance and always bears fruit.

Living from my heart, a deeper way of knowing.
Living from my heart, praising with thanksgiving,
with love.

Living from my heart, giving, forgiving, healing.
Living from my heart, wholeness, forgiveness,
celebration.

Living in fantasy, disconnected from truth, alienated from reality. False living separates me from truth.

Living in truth, I am healed, empowered, moved beyond alienation, and anchored in reality.

Balancing being and doing, life and work, brings
harmony and contentment to every experience;
encourages me to come alive to my true self.

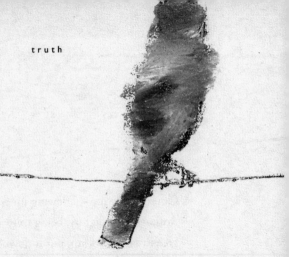

My true self is open, receptive, limitless,
boundless. My true self is unconditionally loved
by God.

Conscious living – knowing inner freedom,
working with dignity, being fully aware.
Free to take work up, put it down, to give
thanks and praise.

I pray for a peaceful death. I pray for a holy
death, death as a celebration, a completion of life.

Life is a gift. A unique expression of God's love.

Feeling unloved, rejected, unvalued, under attack, criticised, afraid, no good, not wanted, I find it hard to love.

Realising I am lovable, accepted, wanted, valued, healed. Loving myself, I love anew.

Truth comes in pairs of opposites.
I am strong when I embrace my weaknesses; I am
a teacher when I can be taught; I enjoy others
when I enjoy myself; I am wise when I accept my
own foolishness; I find true laughter when I laugh
at myself.

As a tree draws its sustenance from the sun, rain and soil, so too we draw sustenance from the source of all life.

Like a tree planted in good soil by flowing waters, I am rooted in love, delighting in God, yielding fruit in due season.

awakening

Waiting, watching, in the still, dark silence, not knowing. Then just before sunrise the world takes in a deep breath, birds awaken, a crescendo of cacophonous twitters salutes the day. Dawn chorus, exhaling new life, echoing over the earth.

awakening

Morning, the womb of life – pregnant with courage, challenge, goodness; seeds of new beginnings.

February, early morning, little rays of light come
seeping in; daybreak in a Dublin church. Dawn
washing through stained-glass windows, a tapestry
of reds, blues and golds, illuminating the glorious
ascent into heaven. An invitation to greet this new
day, witnessing the risen Christ.

Before day breaks upon me, help me set aside
time in the silence of mindfulness and meditation
to guard me, to protect me, to enrich me.

Help me to do what I do well, happily,
joyfully, freely.

Help me to bring a sense of the sacred into the day, carry it like a song in my heart, permeating everything I do, everything I say, everything I am.

Life – my time to bless.
Life – puff of winter cold, flash of a swallow,
sound of a mosquito, shadow across my path,
whispering of wind, scent of hay, cadence of
greeting, singing, welcoming, tissue of a rose, last
glimmer of daylight, first light of dawn,
bud of a snowdrop.
Life – blessings from God.

Every morning, fresh, new, exciting, delightful
as the first creation morning.

I am blessed as I open to the gifts of the day and
savour, relish, rest, rejoice in what I have been
given – the delicious fruits of the spirit.

Before the clatter begins, in silence and solitude,
I hear a new day. Out of silence, gradually I open
my heart, quieten my mind and restore my senses,
as I enter the day with a new awareness.

As dawn crests over the horizon and consecrates
the day, consecrate me anew.

Morning, a call to be awake to everything, in
everything – a kind word, thought,
disappointment, loss, mistake, a new dream,
vision – I am called to see and hear with an
open heart.

Joy cannot be organised, cannot be planned. I need only desire it, seek it and it finds me. Joy transcends what I think I can do, think I can be. Joy always surprises.

All day, every day, I have new moments of
wonder to be grateful for – fresh raindrops, wild
flowers, sunshine, birds nesting, a card from a
friend, conversations, a table tastefully arranged,
an unexpected gift, a smile of welcome.

Reminding me to awaken to the wonders
of the day.

Knowing the happiness of an integrated life, I
bring body, mind and spirit into who I am and
what I do.

Life taken for granted never knows joy.

Early in the morning, help me see all God's love –
supporting, guiding, working in me, with me,
through me. The music of gratitude is available all
day, every day, when I remember to listen.

awakening

In the morning, bless me with the time and space
to be attentive to all that is new. Bless me with the
time and space to give thanks, to go forth with
strength, taking part in the divine design
for the day.

My unawakened mind seeks happiness, searches,
grasps, wants more, is restless, is never satisfied,
is lost.

My awakened mind seeks happiness, stops,
reflects, ponders, knows happiness is here,
is secure.

acceptance

This day; one pulse in the cycle of endings and beginnings, sowing and reaping, planting and harvesting, spring and autumn, morning and evening.

Creation: beginning time, before time, in time, all time.

Creation: ongoing story, new beginnings, nothing complete.

Creation: arising out of emptiness, taking form, returning again to emptiness, in a ceaseless rhythm of new beginnings.

Pacing myself, taking time to be still. Praying,
meditating or listening to music. This restores my
balance, settles me down, allows me to flow with a
natural rhythm, with new belonging.

My restless heart finds refuge in the embrace
of quiet.

Journeying outward – interesting, engaging,
challenging, never fully satisfying.
Journeying inward – slow, painful, leading to my
heart's desire, discovering my true self. A place of
joy, of peace, of hope, of love.

Two journeys, becoming one.
Blessings, peace.

We are creatures of the earth, born to live in
rhythm with nature, rise with the sun, sleep with
the dark, work in light.
However, we move through the day to the rhythm
of timetables, caught up in the need to do what
we think needs doing – another day's unnatural
rhythms.

Insight, the key to a full life, into our true selves.
Give me the insight I need to release all fear and
threat. Open me to honesty, integrity, justice, joy,
transformation, enriching my day.

Giving thanks for myself is a step towards acceptance. I learn to love myself and, through loving myself, I am healed.

Taking time to sit, bless, eat, nourish, digest.
Creating space for me, for others, for all creation.
A way of mindfulness.

Discovering my uniqueness fills me with energy, excitement, motivation. I find a joy I didn't know I was looking for.

Eating and drinking, a political act. Remembering
those who have little food, too much food,
waste food.

Eating and drinking, mindfully I connect to the
whole world as I care for my body, to live, work,
help my neighbour, reverence the universe.

Whatever I do; cook, clean, write, visit, walk, talk, listen, climb, rest, I do anyway. Doing whatever I do lovingly, carefully, attentively, tenderly yet with awareness, always brings inner peace.

Giving and receiving replenishes my energy. It
opens within me a new consciousness, inviting me
to notice, to reciprocate, and creates life anew.

In detachment from things, I am free from
small-mindedness.
In practising wakeful presence, I take possession
of myself.
In letting go, I live with ambiguity.
In living with questions, I wait for answers.

Born to wonder, question, experience, explore.
These are not my special gifts, but part of being
my true self.

Staying close to affluence, my wants increase, vessels enlarge, rarely full, never enough. Staying close to the source of life, my needs diminish, vessels reduce, I am always full, overflowing with joy.

Looking deep within and facing myself, my truth,
my uniqueness, feelings, gifts and failings.
Knowing I am loved, loving and loveable, I am
released from fear, healed of my wounds, I am free
to be myself and I know it brings peace at night.

As a musician, athlete, dancer benefits from the discipline of routine, so too I unfold and blossom with vitality, joy and sensitivity from a daily spiritual routine.

With simplicity, I assent to live close to the limits
of my resources, to recognise needs and wants, to
be satisfied with enough and generous
towards others.

Prayer calls me to healthy self-loving and balanced living. Prayer calls me to depth, security, serenity, tenderness, honesty, trust and compassion. Prayer calls me to be myself every day.

The shadow controls me as long as I reject it, repress it. The shadow accepted frees me to be my true self, to rest in peace.

I am called to make the world a better place,
a more just place, a more meaningful place, a safer
place. It is a call in history, a vocation in time.

A cluttered mind, no space for thinking.
An overburdened heart, no space for relationships.
Emptying my mind, emptying my heart, creates
space for safety, serenity, kindness. Space for
listening, learning, knowing, as the hollow empty
reed leaves space for music.

In the evening of my day, I begin to know truth.
Embracing life, I discover who I am.

Building walls – physical walls, psychological walls, cultural walls, spiritual walls – segregates and divides.

As long as other people are on their own side of the wall, seeing them as walled-off categories, I am safe and secure in my blindness.

Creation; always becoming, never complete.
Always being shaped, never static.
Creation; moulding, fashioning, stripping,
purifying, growing, blossoming, pruning, daring
us to become ourselves.

Accepting my wounded nature releases energy
focused on hurt, making it available as a healing
power for myself, others, the universe.

Tomorrow is the enemy of today. I cannot be tomorrow what I can be today.

False humility deludes me into trying to be what
I am not and prevents me from acknowledging
my gifts and the gift of others.

With true humility, I feel secure in uncertainty;
I own my gifts, recognise the gifts of others, and
give thanks.

Holy time.
Time out of schedules I build to make me feel
safe. Time out of timetables I create to keep me
on track. Time out of routines I impose to give
me the illusion of control. The rhythm of holy
time loosens the chains that bind me, setting me
free, bringing me peace.

acceptance

stillness

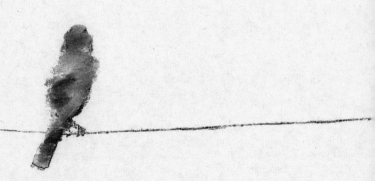

Sabbath; rest, restoration, refreshment, breathing
in, breathing out, thanksgiving, peace, joy.

In keeping the Sabbath we remember everything
has its place, its time. I remember with
tenderness, love, wonder and joy the beauty
of our world, the beauty of my day.

stillness

Blessed with a word, a smile, a kindness, a prayer;
then, blessed by you, I bless on my way.

Stopping. Pausing. Part of the rhythm in Buddhist communities. A mindfulness bell is rung, everyone stops, taking three mindful breaths.

Bell or no bell, stopping brings me to the now of today. Before turning on the computer, opening the door, getting into the car, answering the phone, let me stop, pause and breathe, mindful, still, at peace.

Midday. Angelus bells. Prayer time. An ancient
monastic call to pray – in fields, schools,
hospitals, towns, offices, homes, factories, shops,
cars, buses, trains, planes, on streets. We pause to
pray, pray for peace.

Stopping, I take a moment to become conscious of who I am, bringing together the threads of my history. Reminding me where I have come from, remembering where I am heading, what I am drawn to, why I do what I do.

When enthusiasm flags or crisis looms, when dejection threatens or the challenges of the day are overwhelming, remind me to stop. Call me to reflect, catch my breath, make peace, find joy, take rest, and find strength in the moment.

Making space. Resting in the moment.
Remembering the preciousness of life.
Taking time. Relishing life with joy, with wonder.
Remembering to give thanks.

My world can be buzzing with voices of
aggression, fear, doubt and criticism.

By taking time to listen to my inner voice
in silence, in solitude and in peace, I listen to
my heart's voice, as it is drawn into wisdom.
Taking time to be.

With silence embraced, glimpses of truth and beauty become visible. The wise composer allows music to crescendo, reach a climax and then –

> pause
> a rest
> silence
> nothing.

Listening to silence, I hear the music.

Completing the circle of day, mirroring the flow of life.

Help me let go of the mechanical forces ruling my life.

Remind me to pace myself according to the rhythms of day and night, time and tide, heartbeat, eternity.

Waiting in faith, in silence. Surrendering to darkness, nothingness, emptiness, powerlessness. I find light in darkness, achievement in nothingness, fullness in emptiness, peace in silence, contentment in God.

Stopping. Sitting still helps me to let thoughts go,
to move gently into myself, heart and soul,
connecting with who I am.

The emptiness of silence becomes
inexhaustibly full.

Stopping. Opening myself to the day, blessing,
appreciating, taking note of life's gift.

Stopping. Looking inward, looking outward,
celebrating life.

Stopping. I am present to the source of life,
to the immensity of the divine, to the infinite
touch of love.

In silence and stillness I notice people around me.
The cry of their hearts reminds me who they are,
who I am, where we are going, how we journey
together.

Stepping back and harvesting the gifts of the day.
Reflecting on its fruits, giving thanks. Knowing
the difference between holding and grasping,
needing and wanting, brings peace.

Rushed and hurried, trading happiness for desire,
mindfulness for craving, generosity for jealousy.

Stopping to pray, surrendering my desires and
cravings, taking time to relish my gifts, I give
thanks. Knowing peace, joy, gratitude,
love, freedom.

Silence;
A time to read the signs of our time.
A time to listen to the voices of the poor.
A time to hear in the depths of our hearts.
A time to understand what I am being called to,
what is being asked of me, at this time, in
this place.

Divine blessings, giving life to my inner being,
offering opportunities to recognise my gifts,
realise my potential, live my dreams.
The best that I can be this day is already within.

Doing – the energy to move with focused
attention, accomplish specific tasks, achieve goals.

Being – the energy to ponder, be centred, be fully present in the moment with receptive awareness.

Wholeness – balancing being and doing.

Call me to the simplicity of a child, to live life in the moment, following my energies, connecting with my spirit, without distortion or destruction.

Being connected with the earth roots me in
reality, relieves me from anxieties, self-centredness,
self-importance, and allows me to see myself in
the scheme of things and in the divine plan.

Presence – a sacred experience in stillness.
A healing experience in pain, a comforting
experience in grief, a graced experience in oneness.
A joyful experience in celebration.

Always there for me.

Aware or unaware, I create my own solutions, my
own reality, by choice or by chance.
Aware, I choose inner peace with joy
and confidence.

Inner peace. Outcome of the day I have lived.
Listening with my heart I come to know and give
thanks for colour, smell, touch, sound of the day
and its messages.

Anytime is a time to stop, reflect, accept what has been. Live in the moment. A time to commit to the future with confidence, strength, courage.

At prayer; touching the depths, aware of my
frailty, recognising my brokenness, connecting
with the frailty of all humanity.
Prayer; accepting all that divides, all that unifies,
all that is broken, knowing peace.

Food;
Preparing it, appreciating its smell, taste, colour,
presentation, remembering with love those who
prepared, cooked and served it – a form of
meditation.

A piece of bread, sandwich, slice of fruit, cup of
tea, becomes a sacred meal when taken quietly,
mindfully, alone or with others.

A moment of togetherness, a moment of sharing,
a moment to give thanks, a celebration of fullness.

O Source of Life, the more I gather, store, hoard,
put away, the less I receive. The more I share,
let go, give away, the more I receive.

Tuning into ourselves, into others, requires inner
calm, sharp concentration, deep intuition, an
awareness that remains quiet and clear.
A perspective that is extensive, deep,
broad, focused.

Tuning in to myself – an invitation to silence,
stillness, enabling me to be receptive,
understanding. Perhaps more confused but, in the
end, more fruitful in whatever I do.

Stillness and silence awaits me everywhere. I don't have to travel from the busyness of the city, the bustle of living. I find it when I stop and notice the petal of a flower, a cloud over the sun, the changing moon, the colours of the sea, the perfection of a newborn child, a blanket of snow, the leaves falling, the magic of birdsong, the countless wonders of day and night.

Gifts not given become burdens, harming not
freeing us. Life-taking, not life-giving.

In stillness and silence, help me to experience wisdom. Challenge me to listen, encourage me to take risks, loving me into accepting myself.

Wisdom is waiting to be found, waiting for me to discover, in stillness and in silence, the wonder of who I am.

Being grateful; elevating the ordinary, extending boundaries, removing limits, I am renewed, living with joy, living to the full.

When I am too busy to be still, to be silent, to
notice, I do not see what is around me, I do not
hear what is being spoken in my heart.

Direct me not to become what others tell
me I am:
Masculine – doing, active, rational, strong,
organised, serious, responsible, intellectual.
Feminine – being, passive, intuitive, vulnerable,
spontaneous, spiritual, receptive, emotional.

Help me to listen to the small voice within, when
I will discover the person I am called to be, in my
being, in my doing, in my delightful uniqueness.

Stillness, present in any space, every place,
available, always, everywhere, to all who seek it.

Now is the Time

Spiritual Reflections
Sister Stan

Now is the Time became an instant bestseller when it was first published, and in this expanded edition, which includes five new entries, Stan's message remains the same: we have the time, if we make the choice to take time . . .

Now is the Time is a book for everyone; young or old, male or female, for the converted or those who are irreligious or plain disaffected. Even people for whom a spiritual view of the world is a closed book should try opening this one.

Now is the Time looks beyond the boundaries of any one faith or church and draws on the great spiritual and philosophical traditions of east and west.

As Sister Stan focuses on a line of poetry from one of the world's great authors, an idea from a psychotherapist or philosopher, or a proverb from oriental wisdom, she weaves her own thoughts around them in a way that presents them afresh, and allows us to see them from a new perspective.

Now is the Time is an inspiring and thought-provoking work of vision.

9781848270633

Seasons of the Day

A Book of Hours
Sister Stan

Based on the traditional *Book of Hours* – psalms said daily, at set times, by religious communities throughout the world – *Seasons of the Day* reveals the enduring relevance of this ancient practice to contemporary living.

In *Seasons of the Day*, Sister Stan, knowing that our modern-day understanding of time pushes us to our stressed-out limits, passes on the monastic ritual to the layperson.

Here, as she slows us down, she reveals the psalms through her own words, her own prayers. Using them, she also guides us tenderly through a four-week period, from the silence and mystery of pre-dawn (*matins*) through to the reflective conclusion of the day (*compline*).

In a world that can often seem hostile and unfriendly, Sister Stan's gentle reflections help the reader find inner peace and confidence.

A prayer book for today.

9781848270626

Gardening the Soul

Soothing Seasonal Thoughts for Jaded Modern Souls
Sister Stan

Sister Stan, as she is affectionately known, was brought up on a farm in Dingle, County Kerry, one of the most beautiful parts of Ireland. It was there that she learnt to appreciate the earth, its stillness and its energy, its beauty and its bounty.

In this hugely powerful and evocative book, Sister Stan looks to the earth for inspiration. Reflecting the garden's changing rhythms through the seasons, *Gardening the Soul* offers us a daily thought to keep us going as we face the challenges of modern life.

All our moods are covered here . . .

- in January, when there is silence in the garden, she looks at Solitude in our soul . . .
- in March, with emergence in the garden, she offers Hope . . .
- in August, when there is fullness and abundance everywhere, there is Blessing, and
- in October, the time of harvest, there is Harmony.

Comforting and insightful, *Gardening the Soul* is an inspirational daybook of lessons gleaned from the wisdom of nature.

The *Irish Times* Spiritual Book of the Year, 2002

9781848270640